50 Baking for Every Occasion Recipes

By: Kelly Johnson

Table of Contents

- Classic Chocolate Chip Cookies
- Red Velvet Cake
- Lemon Drizzle Pound Cake
- Banana Bread
- Funfetti Cupcakes
- Cinnamon Rolls
- Pumpkin Pie
- Chocolate Brownies
- Blueberry Muffins
- Vanilla Bean Cheesecake
- Apple Crisp
- Pecan Pie
- Shortbread Cookies
- Tiramisu
- Coconut Macaroons
- Peanut Butter Cookies
- Carrot Cake
- Chocolate Lava Cake
- Strawberry Rhubarb Pie
- Almond Biscotti
- Raspberry Almond Tart
- Zucchini Bread
- Cheesecake Bars
- Gingerbread Cookies
- Scones with Jam and Cream
- Chocolate Soufflé
- Fudge Brownies with Nuts
- Maple Pecan Tarts
- Oatmeal Raisin Cookies
- Key Lime Pie
- Flourless Chocolate Cake
- Fruit Galette
- Honey Almond Cake
- Chocolate Cupcakes with Buttercream Frosting
- Peach Cobbler
- Caramel Apple Tart

- Matcha Green Tea Cookies
- Berry Crumble Bars
- Chocolate Chip Banana Muffins
- Coconut Cream Pie
- Bourbon Pecan Pie
- Espresso Brownies
- Marble Cake
- Vanilla Pudding Cake
- Chocolate Chip Pancakes
- Fruit and Nut Granola Bars
- Buttermilk Biscuits
- Cherry Clafoutis
- Chocolate Hazelnut Torte
- Peanut Butter Pie

Classic Chocolate Chip Cookies

Ingredients

- 1 cup unsalted butter, softened
- 3/4 cup granulated sugar
- 3/4 cup packed brown sugar
- 1 teaspoon vanilla extract
- 2 large eggs
- 2 1/4 cups all-purpose flour
- 1 teaspoon baking soda
- 1/2 teaspoon salt
- 2 cups chocolate chips

Instructions

1. **Preheat Oven:** Preheat your oven to 375°F (190°C).
2. **Mix Ingredients:** In a large bowl, cream together butter, granulated sugar, brown sugar, and vanilla until smooth. Beat in eggs one at a time.
3. **Combine Dry Ingredients:** In another bowl, combine flour, baking soda, and salt. Gradually blend the dry ingredients into the wet mixture. Stir in chocolate chips.
4. **Bake:** Drop by rounded tablespoon onto ungreased baking sheets. Bake for 9-11 minutes or until golden brown.
5. **Cool:** Let cool on baking sheets for a few minutes before transferring to wire racks to cool completely.

Red Velvet Cake

Ingredients

- 2 1/2 cups all-purpose flour
- 1 1/2 cups granulated sugar
- 1 teaspoon baking soda
- 1 teaspoon salt
- 1 teaspoon cocoa powder
- 1 1/2 cups vegetable oil
- 1 cup buttermilk, room temperature
- 2 large eggs, room temperature
- 2 tablespoons red food coloring
- 1 teaspoon vanilla extract
- 1 teaspoon white vinegar

Instructions

1. **Preheat Oven:** Preheat your oven to 350°F (175°C). Grease and flour two 9-inch round cake pans.
2. **Combine Dry Ingredients:** In a bowl, whisk together flour, sugar, baking soda, salt, and cocoa powder.
3. **Mix Wet Ingredients:** In another bowl, mix oil, buttermilk, eggs, food coloring, vanilla, and vinegar.
4. **Combine:** Gradually mix the dry ingredients into the wet mixture until smooth.
5. **Bake:** Pour batter into prepared pans and bake for 25-30 minutes. Let cool in pans for 10 minutes, then transfer to wire racks to cool completely.

Lemon Drizzle Pound Cake

Ingredients

- 1 cup unsalted butter, softened
- 2 cups granulated sugar
- 4 large eggs
- 3 cups all-purpose flour
- 1 teaspoon baking powder
- 1/2 teaspoon salt
- 1 cup buttermilk
- Zest of 2 lemons
- 1/4 cup fresh lemon juice

Instructions

1. **Preheat Oven:** Preheat your oven to 350°F (175°C). Grease a 9x5-inch loaf pan.
2. **Cream Butter and Sugar:** In a large bowl, cream together butter and sugar until light and fluffy. Beat in eggs one at a time.
3. **Mix Dry Ingredients:** In another bowl, combine flour, baking powder, and salt.
4. **Combine Mixtures:** Gradually mix the dry ingredients into the butter mixture alternately with buttermilk, starting and ending with flour. Stir in lemon zest and juice.
5. **Bake:** Pour batter into prepared loaf pan and bake for 60-70 minutes. Let cool in the pan for 10 minutes before transferring to a wire rack.

Banana Bread

Ingredients

- 1/2 cup unsalted butter, softened
- 1 cup granulated sugar
- 2 large eggs
- 4 ripe bananas, mashed
- 1 teaspoon vanilla extract
- 1 1/2 cups all-purpose flour
- 1 teaspoon baking soda
- 1/4 teaspoon salt
- 1/2 teaspoon cinnamon (optional)

Instructions

1. **Preheat Oven:** Preheat your oven to 350°F (175°C). Grease a 9x5-inch loaf pan.
2. **Cream Butter and Sugar:** In a large bowl, cream together butter and sugar until smooth. Beat in eggs, bananas, and vanilla.
3. **Combine Dry Ingredients:** In another bowl, combine flour, baking soda, salt, and cinnamon (if using).
4. **Combine Mixtures:** Gradually mix the dry ingredients into the wet mixture until just combined.
5. **Bake:** Pour batter into prepared loaf pan and bake for 60-70 minutes. Let cool in the pan for 10 minutes before transferring to a wire rack.

Funfetti Cupcakes

Ingredients

- 1 1/2 cups all-purpose flour
- 1 cup granulated sugar
- 1/2 cup unsalted butter, softened
- 2 large eggs
- 1/2 cup milk
- 1 teaspoon vanilla extract
- 2 teaspoons baking powder
- 1/4 teaspoon salt
- 1/2 cup rainbow sprinkles

Instructions

1. **Preheat Oven:** Preheat your oven to 350°F (175°C). Line a cupcake pan with liners.
2. **Mix Ingredients:** In a large bowl, cream together butter and sugar until fluffy. Beat in eggs one at a time, then stir in milk and vanilla.
3. **Combine Dry Ingredients:** In another bowl, combine flour, baking powder, and salt. Gradually mix dry ingredients into the wet mixture until just combined.
4. **Add Sprinkles:** Fold in the rainbow sprinkles.
5. **Bake:** Fill cupcake liners about 2/3 full and bake for 15-20 minutes. Let cool before frosting.

Cinnamon Rolls

Ingredients

- 4 cups all-purpose flour
- 1/4 cup granulated sugar
- 1 packet (2 1/4 teaspoons) active dry yeast
- 1 teaspoon salt
- 1 cup milk, warmed
- 1/4 cup unsalted butter, melted
- 2 large eggs
- 1 tablespoon cinnamon
- 1/2 cup brown sugar

Instructions

1. **Prepare Dough:** In a bowl, mix flour, sugar, yeast, and salt. In another bowl, combine milk, melted butter, and eggs. Mix wet ingredients into dry ingredients until a dough forms.
2. **Knead Dough:** Knead on a floured surface for about 5 minutes until smooth. Place in a greased bowl and let rise for 1 hour.
3. **Roll and Fill:** Roll dough into a rectangle, spread with softened butter, sprinkle with brown sugar and cinnamon. Roll up tightly and cut into slices.
4. **Bake:** Place rolls in a greased baking dish and let rise for 30 minutes. Preheat oven to 375°F (190°C) and bake for 20-25 minutes.

Pumpkin Pie

Ingredients

- 1 (9-inch) pie crust
- 1 can (15 oz) pumpkin puree
- 3/4 cup granulated sugar
- 1 teaspoon cinnamon
- 1/2 teaspoon nutmeg
- 1/4 teaspoon ginger
- 1/4 teaspoon salt
- 3 large eggs
- 1 can (12 oz) evaporated milk

Instructions

1. **Preheat Oven:** Preheat your oven to 425°F (220°C).
2. **Mix Ingredients:** In a large bowl, combine pumpkin, sugar, spices, and salt. Beat in eggs, then gradually mix in evaporated milk.
3. **Prepare Pie Crust:** Pour filling into the pie crust.
4. **Bake:** Bake for 15 minutes, then reduce the temperature to 350°F (175°C) and bake for an additional 40-50 minutes, or until set.

Chocolate Brownies

Ingredients

- 1/2 cup unsalted butter
- 1 cup granulated sugar
- 2 large eggs
- 1 teaspoon vanilla extract
- 1/3 cup cocoa powder
- 1/2 cup all-purpose flour
- 1/4 teaspoon salt
- 1/4 teaspoon baking powder

Instructions

1. **Preheat Oven:** Preheat your oven to 350°F (175°C). Grease an 8x8-inch baking pan.
2. **Melt Butter:** In a saucepan, melt butter. Remove from heat and stir in sugar, eggs, and vanilla.
3. **Combine Dry Ingredients:** Stir in cocoa, flour, salt, and baking powder until well combined.
4. **Bake:** Spread batter into the prepared pan and bake for 20-25 minutes. Let cool before cutting into squares.

Blueberry Muffins

Ingredients

- 2 cups all-purpose flour
- 1/2 cup granulated sugar
- 2 teaspoons baking powder
- 1/2 teaspoon salt
- 1/2 cup unsalted butter, melted
- 1 cup milk
- 2 large eggs
- 1 teaspoon vanilla extract
- 1 1/2 cups fresh blueberries

Instructions

1. **Preheat Oven:** Preheat your oven to 375°F (190°C). Line a muffin tin with paper liners.
2. **Mix Dry Ingredients:** In a large bowl, whisk together flour, sugar, baking powder, and salt.
3. **Mix Wet Ingredients:** In another bowl, combine melted butter, milk, eggs, and vanilla.
4. **Combine Mixtures:** Pour the wet ingredients into the dry ingredients and stir until just combined. Gently fold in blueberries.
5. **Bake:** Divide the batter among the muffin cups and bake for 20-25 minutes, or until a toothpick comes out clean.

Vanilla Bean Cheesecake

Ingredients

- 1 1/2 cups graham cracker crumbs
- 1/4 cup sugar
- 1/2 cup unsalted butter, melted
- 4 (8 oz) packages cream cheese, softened
- 1 cup granulated sugar
- 4 large eggs
- 1 tablespoon vanilla extract
- 1 vanilla bean, split and seeds scraped

Instructions

1. **Preheat Oven:** Preheat your oven to 325°F (160°C). Grease a 9-inch springform pan.
2. **Prepare Crust:** In a bowl, combine graham cracker crumbs, sugar, and melted butter. Press mixture into the bottom of the prepared pan.
3. **Mix Filling:** In a large bowl, beat cream cheese and sugar until smooth. Add eggs one at a time, mixing well after each addition. Stir in vanilla extract and vanilla bean seeds.
4. **Bake:** Pour filling over crust and bake for 55-60 minutes. Turn off the oven and let cheesecake cool in the oven for 1 hour.
5. **Chill:** Refrigerate for at least 4 hours before serving.

Apple Crisp

Ingredients

- 6 cups sliced apples (about 6 apples)
- 1 tablespoon lemon juice
- 3/4 cup granulated sugar
- 1 teaspoon ground cinnamon
- 1 cup rolled oats
- 1 cup all-purpose flour
- 1/2 cup brown sugar
- 1/2 cup unsalted butter, softened

Instructions

1. **Preheat Oven:** Preheat your oven to 350°F (175°C). Grease a 9x13-inch baking dish.
2. **Prepare Apples:** In a bowl, toss sliced apples with lemon juice, granulated sugar, and cinnamon. Spread mixture in the baking dish.
3. **Make Topping:** In another bowl, combine oats, flour, brown sugar, and softened butter. Mix until crumbly.
4. **Assemble:** Sprinkle topping over apples.
5. **Bake:** Bake for 30-35 minutes or until topping is golden brown and apples are tender.

Pecan Pie

Ingredients

- 1 unbaked pie crust
- 1 cup corn syrup
- 1 cup granulated sugar
- 1/2 cup unsalted butter, melted
- 4 large eggs
- 1 teaspoon vanilla extract
- 1 1/2 cups pecans

Instructions

1. **Preheat Oven:** Preheat your oven to 350°F (175°C).
2. **Mix Filling:** In a large bowl, combine corn syrup, sugar, melted butter, eggs, and vanilla. Stir until well mixed.
3. **Add Pecans:** Stir in pecans and pour mixture into the pie crust.
4. **Bake:** Bake for 60-70 minutes or until the filling is set.
5. **Cool:** Allow to cool before slicing.

Shortbread Cookies

Ingredients

- 2 cups unsalted butter, softened
- 1 cup granulated sugar
- 4 cups all-purpose flour
- 1 teaspoon vanilla extract
- 1/4 teaspoon salt

Instructions

1. **Preheat Oven:** Preheat your oven to 325°F (160°C).
2. **Cream Butter and Sugar:** In a large bowl, cream together butter and sugar until light and fluffy.
3. **Add Dry Ingredients:** Gradually mix in flour and salt until combined. Stir in vanilla.
4. **Shape Cookies:** Roll dough into logs or cut into shapes. Place on ungreased baking sheets.
5. **Bake:** Bake for 20-25 minutes or until lightly golden.

Tiramisu

Ingredients

- 1 cup brewed espresso, cooled
- 1/2 cup coffee liqueur (optional)
- 3 large eggs, separated
- 3/4 cup granulated sugar
- 8 oz mascarpone cheese
- 1 cup heavy cream
- 24 ladyfinger cookies
- Cocoa powder for dusting

Instructions

1. **Combine Espresso and Liqueur:** In a shallow dish, combine espresso and coffee liqueur.
2. **Mix Egg Yolks and Sugar:** In a bowl, whisk egg yolks and sugar until thick and pale. Add mascarpone and mix until smooth.
3. **Whip Egg Whites:** In another bowl, beat egg whites until stiff peaks form. Fold into the mascarpone mixture.
4. **Whip Cream:** In another bowl, whip heavy cream until stiff peaks form. Fold into the egg mixture.
5. **Layer:** Dip ladyfingers in the espresso mixture and layer in a dish. Spread half the mascarpone mixture over them. Repeat layers.
6. **Chill:** Refrigerate for at least 4 hours, then dust with cocoa powder before serving.

Coconut Macaroons

Ingredients

- 2 2/3 cups sweetened shredded coconut
- 1/2 cup sweetened condensed milk
- 1 teaspoon vanilla extract
- 2 large egg whites
- 1/4 teaspoon salt

Instructions

1. **Preheat Oven:** Preheat your oven to 325°F (160°C). Line a baking sheet with parchment paper.
2. **Mix Ingredients:** In a bowl, combine coconut, sweetened condensed milk, vanilla, egg whites, and salt.
3. **Form Cookies:** Drop spoonfuls of the mixture onto the prepared baking sheet.
4. **Bake:** Bake for 20-25 minutes or until golden brown. Allow to cool on the baking sheet.

Peanut Butter Cookies

Ingredients

- 1 cup peanut butter
- 1 cup granulated sugar
- 1 large egg
- 1 teaspoon baking soda
- 1/4 teaspoon salt

Instructions

1. **Preheat Oven:** Preheat your oven to 350°F (175°C).
2. **Mix Ingredients:** In a bowl, combine peanut butter, sugar, egg, baking soda, and salt until well blended.
3. **Form Cookies:** Roll into balls and place on a baking sheet. Flatten each ball with a fork, making a crisscross pattern.
4. **Bake:** Bake for 10-12 minutes or until lightly browned. Let cool on the baking sheet.

Carrot Cake

Ingredients

- 2 cups all-purpose flour
- 2 cups granulated sugar
- 1 teaspoon baking powder
- 1 teaspoon baking soda
- 1 teaspoon ground cinnamon
- 1/2 teaspoon salt
- 1 cup vegetable oil
- 4 large eggs
- 3 cups grated carrots
- 1 cup crushed pineapple, drained
- 1/2 cup chopped walnuts (optional)

Instructions

1. **Preheat Oven:** Preheat your oven to 350°F (175°C). Grease and flour two 9-inch round cake pans.
2. **Mix Dry Ingredients:** In a large bowl, whisk together flour, sugar, baking powder, baking soda, cinnamon, and salt.
3. **Mix Wet Ingredients:** In another bowl, beat together oil and eggs. Stir in grated carrots and crushed pineapple.
4. **Combine Mixtures:** Add the wet ingredients to the dry ingredients and mix until just combined. Fold in walnuts if using.
5. **Bake:** Divide batter between the prepared pans and bake for 25-30 minutes, or until a toothpick comes out clean.
6. **Cool:** Allow to cool in the pans for 10 minutes before transferring to wire racks to cool completely.

Chocolate Lava Cake

Ingredients

- 1/2 cup unsalted butter
- 1 cup semi-sweet chocolate chips
- 2 large eggs
- 2 large egg yolks
- 1/4 cup granulated sugar
- 2 tablespoons all-purpose flour
- 1/4 teaspoon salt

Instructions

1. **Preheat Oven:** Preheat your oven to 425°F (220°C). Grease four ramekins.
2. **Melt Butter and Chocolate:** In a microwave-safe bowl, melt butter and chocolate together until smooth.
3. **Mix Ingredients:** In another bowl, whisk together eggs, egg yolks, and sugar until thick. Stir in chocolate mixture, then fold in flour and salt.
4. **Fill Ramekins:** Pour batter into prepared ramekins and place them on a baking sheet.
5. **Bake:** Bake for 12-14 minutes until the edges are firm but the center is soft.
6. **Serve:** Let cool for 1 minute, then invert onto plates and serve immediately.

Strawberry Rhubarb Pie

Ingredients

- 1 double pie crust (store-bought or homemade)
- 2 cups sliced strawberries
- 2 cups sliced rhubarb
- 1 1/4 cups granulated sugar
- 1/4 cup cornstarch
- 1 teaspoon vanilla extract
- 1 tablespoon lemon juice
- 1 tablespoon butter, cut into small pieces

Instructions

1. **Preheat Oven:** Preheat your oven to 425°F (220°C).
2. **Prepare Filling:** In a bowl, combine strawberries, rhubarb, sugar, cornstarch, vanilla, and lemon juice.
3. **Assemble Pie:** Place one crust in a pie dish, fill with fruit mixture, and dot with butter. Cover with the second crust, sealing and cutting slits for steam.
4. **Bake:** Bake for 15 minutes at 425°F, then reduce to 350°F (175°C) and bake for an additional 30-35 minutes, until the filling is bubbly.
5. **Cool:** Let cool before slicing.

Almond Biscotti

Ingredients

- 2 cups all-purpose flour
- 1 cup granulated sugar
- 1 teaspoon baking powder
- 1/4 teaspoon salt
- 1/2 cup unsalted butter, softened
- 2 large eggs
- 1 teaspoon almond extract
- 1 cup sliced almonds

Instructions

1. **Preheat Oven:** Preheat your oven to 350°F (175°C). Line a baking sheet with parchment paper.
2. **Mix Ingredients:** In a bowl, mix flour, sugar, baking powder, and salt. In another bowl, cream together butter, eggs, and almond extract.
3. **Combine Mixtures:** Gradually add dry ingredients to wet ingredients, then fold in almonds.
4. **Shape Dough:** Shape the dough into a log and place it on the baking sheet.
5. **Bake:** Bake for 25-30 minutes, then let cool for 10 minutes. Slice into pieces and bake again for 10-15 minutes until golden brown.

Raspberry Almond Tart

Ingredients

- 1 cup all-purpose flour
- 1/4 cup powdered sugar
- 1/2 cup unsalted butter, softened
- 1 large egg yolk
- 1 cup almond flour
- 1/2 cup granulated sugar
- 2 large eggs
- 1 teaspoon almond extract
- 1 cup fresh raspberries

Instructions

1. **Preheat Oven:** Preheat your oven to 350°F (175°C). Grease a tart pan.
2. **Prepare Crust:** In a bowl, combine flour, powdered sugar, and butter. Mix until crumbly. Add egg yolk and mix until dough forms. Press into the tart pan.
3. **Pre-Bake:** Bake crust for 10 minutes, then set aside to cool.
4. **Prepare Filling:** In another bowl, mix almond flour, granulated sugar, eggs, and almond extract. Pour over the crust.
5. **Add Raspberries:** Arrange raspberries on top.
6. **Bake:** Bake for 30-35 minutes until set. Let cool before slicing.

Zucchini Bread

Ingredients

- 2 cups all-purpose flour
- 1 teaspoon baking soda
- 1 teaspoon baking powder
- 1 teaspoon ground cinnamon
- 1/2 teaspoon salt
- 1/2 cup vegetable oil
- 1 cup granulated sugar
- 2 large eggs
- 2 cups grated zucchini
- 1 teaspoon vanilla extract
- 1/2 cup chopped walnuts (optional)

Instructions

1. **Preheat Oven:** Preheat your oven to 350°F (175°C). Grease a 9x5-inch loaf pan.
2. **Mix Dry Ingredients:** In a bowl, whisk together flour, baking soda, baking powder, cinnamon, and salt.
3. **Mix Wet Ingredients:** In another bowl, mix oil, sugar, eggs, zucchini, and vanilla until combined.
4. **Combine Mixtures:** Add dry ingredients to the wet ingredients and mix until just combined. Fold in walnuts if using.
5. **Bake:** Pour batter into the prepared pan and bake for 50-60 minutes, or until a toothpick comes out clean.
6. **Cool:** Let cool in the pan for 10 minutes, then transfer to a wire rack.

Cheesecake Bars

Ingredients

- 1 1/2 cups graham cracker crumbs
- 1/2 cup granulated sugar
- 1/2 cup unsalted butter, melted
- 2 (8 oz) packages cream cheese, softened
- 1/2 cup granulated sugar
- 2 large eggs
- 1 teaspoon vanilla extract

Instructions

1. **Preheat Oven:** Preheat your oven to 325°F (160°C). Grease an 8x8-inch baking dish.
2. **Prepare Crust:** In a bowl, combine graham cracker crumbs, sugar, and melted butter. Press mixture into the bottom of the baking dish.
3. **Mix Filling:** In another bowl, beat cream cheese and sugar until smooth. Add eggs and vanilla and mix until combined.
4. **Bake:** Pour filling over the crust and bake for 30-35 minutes, or until set.
5. **Cool:** Allow to cool, then refrigerate for at least 2 hours before cutting into bars.

Gingerbread Cookies

Ingredients

- 3 cups all-purpose flour
- 1 tablespoon ground ginger
- 1 tablespoon ground cinnamon
- 1/2 teaspoon ground cloves
- 1/2 teaspoon baking soda
- 1/2 teaspoon salt
- 3/4 cup unsalted butter, softened
- 1 cup brown sugar, packed
- 1/2 cup molasses
- 1 large egg

Instructions

1. **Preheat Oven:** Preheat your oven to 350°F (175°C). Line baking sheets with parchment paper.
2. **Mix Dry Ingredients:** In a bowl, whisk together flour, ginger, cinnamon, cloves, baking soda, and salt.
3. **Cream Butter and Sugar:** In another bowl, beat the butter and brown sugar until light and fluffy. Add molasses and egg, mixing well.
4. **Combine Mixtures:** Gradually add the dry ingredients to the wet mixture, mixing until combined.
5. **Roll and Cut:** Roll out the dough to about 1/4 inch thick. Cut into desired shapes and place on the baking sheets.
6. **Bake:** Bake for 8-10 minutes until edges are firm. Allow to cool before decorating.

Scones with Jam and Cream

Ingredients

- 2 cups all-purpose flour
- 1/4 cup granulated sugar
- 1 tablespoon baking powder
- 1/2 teaspoon salt
- 1/2 cup unsalted butter, cold and cubed
- 3/4 cup heavy cream
- 1 large egg
- Jam and clotted cream for serving

Instructions

1. **Preheat Oven:** Preheat your oven to 400°F (200°C). Line a baking sheet with parchment paper.
2. **Mix Dry Ingredients:** In a bowl, combine flour, sugar, baking powder, and salt.
3. **Cut in Butter:** Add the cold butter and mix until the mixture resembles coarse crumbs.
4. **Combine Wet Ingredients:** In another bowl, whisk together cream and egg. Add to the dry mixture and stir until just combined.
5. **Shape and Cut:** Turn the dough onto a floured surface, pat into a circle, and cut into wedges.
6. **Bake:** Place on the baking sheet and bake for 15-20 minutes until golden. Serve warm with jam and cream.

Chocolate Soufflé

Ingredients

- 2 tablespoons unsalted butter, plus more for greasing
- 1/3 cup granulated sugar, plus more for dusting
- 4 ounces semi-sweet chocolate, chopped
- 3 large eggs, separated
- 1/2 teaspoon vanilla extract
- Pinch of salt

Instructions

1. **Preheat Oven:** Preheat your oven to 375°F (190°C). Grease four ramekins with butter and dust with sugar.
2. **Melt Chocolate:** In a saucepan, melt chocolate and 2 tablespoons of butter over low heat, stirring until smooth.
3. **Whisk Egg Yolks:** In a bowl, whisk together egg yolks, vanilla, and melted chocolate until combined.
4. **Beat Egg Whites:** In another bowl, beat egg whites and salt until soft peaks form. Gradually add sugar and continue beating until stiff peaks form.
5. **Combine Mixtures:** Gently fold a third of the egg whites into the chocolate mixture, then fold in the remaining egg whites.
6. **Bake:** Pour the mixture into the ramekins and bake for 12-15 minutes until puffed. Serve immediately.

Fudge Brownies with Nuts

Ingredients

- 1/2 cup unsalted butter
- 1 cup granulated sugar
- 2 large eggs
- 1 teaspoon vanilla extract
- 1/3 cup unsweetened cocoa powder
- 1/2 cup all-purpose flour
- 1/4 teaspoon salt
- 1/4 teaspoon baking powder
- 1/2 cup chopped nuts (walnuts or pecans)

Instructions

1. **Preheat Oven:** Preheat your oven to 350°F (175°C). Grease an 8x8-inch baking dish.
2. **Melt Butter:** In a saucepan, melt butter over low heat. Remove from heat and stir in sugar, eggs, and vanilla.
3. **Mix Dry Ingredients:** In another bowl, combine cocoa, flour, salt, and baking powder. Gradually add to the butter mixture, stirring until just combined.
4. **Add Nuts:** Fold in the chopped nuts.
5. **Bake:** Pour batter into the prepared baking dish and bake for 20-25 minutes. Let cool before cutting into squares.

Maple Pecan Tarts

Ingredients

- 1 1/2 cups pecans, chopped
- 1/2 cup maple syrup
- 1/4 cup brown sugar, packed
- 1/4 cup unsalted butter, melted
- 2 large eggs
- 1 teaspoon vanilla extract
- 1 pre-made pie crust

Instructions

1. **Preheat Oven:** Preheat your oven to 350°F (175°C).
2. **Prepare Filling:** In a bowl, combine chopped pecans, maple syrup, brown sugar, melted butter, eggs, and vanilla until well mixed.
3. **Assemble Tarts:** Roll out the pie crust and cut into circles. Fit into a muffin tin.
4. **Fill Tarts:** Spoon the pecan filling into each crust.
5. **Bake:** Bake for 20-25 minutes until filling is set. Let cool before serving.

Oatmeal Raisin Cookies

Ingredients

- 1 cup unsalted butter, softened
- 1 cup brown sugar, packed
- 1/2 cup granulated sugar
- 2 large eggs
- 1 teaspoon vanilla extract
- 1 1/2 cups all-purpose flour
- 1 teaspoon baking soda
- 1 teaspoon cinnamon
- 3 cups rolled oats
- 1 cup raisins

Instructions

1. **Preheat Oven:** Preheat your oven to 350°F (175°C). Line baking sheets with parchment paper.
2. **Cream Butter and Sugars:** In a large bowl, cream together butter, brown sugar, and granulated sugar until smooth. Add eggs and vanilla, mixing well.
3. **Mix Dry Ingredients:** In another bowl, whisk together flour, baking soda, and cinnamon. Gradually add to the wet mixture.
4. **Add Oats and Raisins:** Stir in oats and raisins until evenly combined.
5. **Bake:** Drop spoonfuls of dough onto the prepared baking sheets and bake for 10-12 minutes until edges are golden.

Key Lime Pie

Ingredients

- 1 1/2 cups graham cracker crumbs
- 1/2 cup granulated sugar
- 1/2 cup unsalted butter, melted
- 4 large egg yolks
- 1 can (14 oz) sweetened condensed milk
- 1/2 cup key lime juice
- 1 teaspoon lime zest
- Whipped cream for serving

Instructions

1. **Preheat Oven:** Preheat your oven to 350°F (175°C).
2. **Prepare Crust:** In a bowl, mix graham cracker crumbs, sugar, and melted butter. Press into the bottom and sides of a pie dish.
3. **Bake Crust:** Bake the crust for 8-10 minutes until lightly golden.
4. **Mix Filling:** In another bowl, whisk together egg yolks, sweetened condensed milk, key lime juice, and lime zest until smooth.
5. **Fill Crust:** Pour filling into the baked crust and bake for an additional 10-15 minutes.
6. **Cool and Serve:** Let cool, then refrigerate before serving with whipped cream.

Flourless Chocolate Cake

Ingredients

- 1 cup semi-sweet chocolate chips
- 1/2 cup unsalted butter
- 3/4 cup granulated sugar
- 3 large eggs
- 1 teaspoon vanilla extract
- 1/2 cup unsweetened cocoa powder
- Pinch of salt

Instructions

1. **Preheat Oven:** Preheat your oven to 375°F (190°C). Grease an 8-inch round cake pan.
2. **Melt Chocolate and Butter:** In a saucepan, melt chocolate and butter over low heat, stirring until smooth.
3. **Mix Ingredients:** Remove from heat and stir in sugar, then eggs one at a time. Mix in vanilla, cocoa powder, and salt until combined.
4. **Bake:** Pour batter into the prepared pan and bake for 25 minutes. Let cool in the pan for 10 minutes before transferring to a wire rack.
5. **Serve:** Dust with powdered sugar before serving.

Fruit Galette

Ingredients

- 1 1/2 cups all-purpose flour
- 1/2 teaspoon salt
- 1/4 cup granulated sugar
- 1/2 cup unsalted butter, cold and cubed
- 4-5 tablespoons ice water
- 2 cups mixed seasonal fruit (e.g., peaches, berries, apples)
- 1 tablespoon cornstarch
- 1 tablespoon lemon juice
- 1 tablespoon brown sugar (for topping)
- 1 egg (for egg wash)

Instructions

1. **Make the Dough:** In a bowl, combine flour, salt, and sugar. Cut in the butter until the mixture resembles coarse crumbs. Gradually add ice water until dough forms. Shape into a disk, wrap in plastic, and refrigerate for at least 30 minutes.
2. **Prepare the Filling:** In another bowl, combine mixed fruit, cornstarch, lemon juice, and brown sugar. Set aside.
3. **Preheat Oven:** Preheat your oven to 375°F (190°C). Line a baking sheet with parchment paper.
4. **Roll Out the Dough:** On a floured surface, roll out the dough into a circle about 12 inches in diameter. Transfer to the baking sheet.
5. **Add Filling:** Place the fruit mixture in the center of the dough, leaving a 2-inch border. Fold the edges over the fruit, pleating as you go.
6. **Egg Wash:** Beat the egg and brush it over the crust.
7. **Bake:** Bake for 35-40 minutes until the crust is golden and the fruit is bubbly. Let cool before serving.

Honey Almond Cake

Ingredients

- 1 cup almond flour
- 1 cup all-purpose flour
- 1 teaspoon baking powder
- 1/2 teaspoon baking soda
- 1/4 teaspoon salt
- 1/2 cup unsalted butter, softened
- 3/4 cup granulated sugar
- 3/4 cup honey
- 3 large eggs
- 1 teaspoon vanilla extract
- 1/2 cup milk

Instructions

1. **Preheat Oven:** Preheat your oven to 350°F (175°C). Grease a 9-inch round cake pan.
2. **Mix Dry Ingredients:** In a bowl, whisk together almond flour, all-purpose flour, baking powder, baking soda, and salt.
3. **Cream Butter and Sugar:** In another bowl, cream together butter, granulated sugar, and honey until smooth. Add eggs, one at a time, mixing well after each addition.
4. **Combine Mixtures:** Gradually add the dry ingredients to the wet mixture, alternating with milk and vanilla. Mix until just combined.
5. **Bake:** Pour the batter into the prepared cake pan and bake for 30-35 minutes until a toothpick comes out clean. Let cool before serving.

Chocolate Cupcakes with Buttercream Frosting

Ingredients

- **For the Cupcakes:**
    - 1 3/4 cups all-purpose flour
    - 1 cup granulated sugar
    - 3/4 cup unsweetened cocoa powder
    - 1 teaspoon baking soda
    - 1/2 teaspoon baking powder
    - 1/2 teaspoon salt
    - 1 cup buttermilk
    - 1/2 cup vegetable oil
    - 2 large eggs
    - 2 teaspoons vanilla extract
    - 1 cup boiling water
- **For the Buttercream Frosting:**
    - 1 cup unsalted butter, softened
    - 4 cups powdered sugar
    - 1/4 cup heavy cream
    - 1 teaspoon vanilla extract

Instructions

1. **Preheat Oven:** Preheat your oven to 350°F (175°C). Line a cupcake pan with paper liners.
2. **Mix Dry Ingredients:** In a large bowl, combine flour, sugar, cocoa powder, baking soda, baking powder, and salt.
3. **Combine Wet Ingredients:** In another bowl, mix buttermilk, oil, eggs, and vanilla. Gradually add to the dry mixture, mixing until combined. Stir in boiling water until smooth.
4. **Bake:** Fill cupcake liners about 2/3 full with batter. Bake for 15-18 minutes, or until a toothpick comes out clean. Let cool completely.
5. **Make Frosting:** In a bowl, beat softened butter until creamy. Gradually add powdered sugar, mixing well. Add heavy cream and vanilla, beating until fluffy.
6. **Frost Cupcakes:** Once cupcakes are cool, frost with buttercream.

Peach Cobbler

Ingredients

- 4 cups fresh peaches, peeled and sliced
- 1 cup granulated sugar (divided)
- 1/2 cup unsalted butter, melted
- 1 cup all-purpose flour
- 1 tablespoon baking powder
- 1/2 teaspoon salt
- 1 cup milk
- 1 teaspoon vanilla extract
- 1 teaspoon ground cinnamon

Instructions

1. **Preheat Oven:** Preheat your oven to 350°F (175°C).
2. **Prepare Peaches:** In a bowl, mix sliced peaches with 1/2 cup sugar and set aside.
3. **Make Batter:** In another bowl, whisk together flour, baking powder, salt, and the remaining sugar. Add melted butter, milk, and vanilla, stirring until smooth.
4. **Assemble Cobbler:** Pour batter into a greased 9x13-inch baking dish. Spoon peaches over the batter, allowing the juices to spread.
5. **Bake:** Sprinkle with cinnamon and bake for 40-45 minutes until golden brown and bubbly. Let cool slightly before serving.

Caramel Apple Tart

Ingredients

- **For the Crust:**
    - 1 1/4 cups all-purpose flour
    - 1/2 cup unsalted butter, cold and cubed
    - 1/4 cup powdered sugar
    - 1/4 teaspoon salt
    - 1 egg yolk
    - 2-3 tablespoons cold water
- **For the Filling:**
    - 3 cups thinly sliced apples (e.g., Granny Smith)
    - 1/4 cup granulated sugar
    - 1/2 teaspoon cinnamon
    - 1/4 cup caramel sauce

Instructions

1. **Preheat Oven:** Preheat your oven to 375°F (190°C).
2. **Make the Crust:** In a bowl, combine flour, butter, powdered sugar, and salt until crumbly. Add egg yolk and cold water until dough forms. Press into a tart pan and chill for 30 minutes.
3. **Prepare Apples:** In a bowl, toss sliced apples with sugar and cinnamon.
4. **Assemble Tart:** Spread caramel sauce over the crust, then arrange apples on top.
5. **Bake:** Bake for 35-40 minutes until apples are tender and crust is golden. Let cool before serving.

Matcha Green Tea Cookies

Ingredients

- 1 cup all-purpose flour
- 1/2 cup almond flour
- 2 tablespoons matcha powder
- 1/2 teaspoon baking powder
- 1/4 teaspoon salt
- 1/2 cup unsalted butter, softened
- 3/4 cup granulated sugar
- 1 large egg
- 1 teaspoon vanilla extract

Instructions

1. **Preheat Oven:** Preheat your oven to 350°F (175°C). Line a baking sheet with parchment paper.
2. **Mix Dry Ingredients:** In a bowl, whisk together all-purpose flour, almond flour, matcha powder, baking powder, and salt.
3. **Cream Butter and Sugar:** In another bowl, cream together butter and sugar until light and fluffy. Beat in the egg and vanilla.
4. **Combine Mixtures:** Gradually add the dry mixture to the wet mixture until just combined.
5. **Bake:** Drop spoonfuls of dough onto the prepared baking sheet and bake for 10-12 minutes. Let cool before serving.

Berry Crumble Bars

Ingredients

- **For the Crust:**
    - 1 1/2 cups all-purpose flour
    - 1/2 cup rolled oats
    - 1/2 cup brown sugar
    - 1/2 cup unsalted butter, melted
    - 1/4 teaspoon salt
- **For the Filling:**
    - 2 cups mixed berries (fresh or frozen)
    - 1/4 cup granulated sugar
    - 1 tablespoon cornstarch
    - 1 tablespoon lemon juice

Instructions

1. **Preheat Oven:** Preheat your oven to 350°F (175°C). Line an 8x8-inch baking dish with parchment paper.
2. **Make Crust:** In a bowl, mix flour, oats, brown sugar, melted butter, and salt until crumbly. Press half of the mixture into the bottom of the baking dish.
3. **Prepare Filling:** In another bowl, combine berries, granulated sugar, cornstarch, and lemon juice.
4. **Assemble Bars:** Spread the berry mixture over the crust. Crumble the remaining mixture over the top.
5. **Bake:** Bake for 30-35 minutes until golden brown. Let cool before cutting into bars.

Chocolate Chip Banana Muffins

Ingredients

- 2 ripe bananas, mashed
- 1/3 cup melted butter
- 1/2 cup granulated sugar
- 1 egg, beaten
- 1 teaspoon vanilla extract
- 1 teaspoon baking soda
- 1/4 teaspoon salt
- 1 cup all-purpose flour
- 1/2 cup chocolate chips

Instructions

1. **Preheat Oven:** Preheat your oven to 350°F (175°C). Line a muffin tin with paper liners.
2. **Combine Ingredients:** In a bowl, mix mashed bananas with melted butter. Stir in sugar, egg, and vanilla. Add baking soda and salt. Gradually mix in flour until just combined.
3. **Add Chocolate Chips:** Fold in chocolate chips.
4. **Bake:** Pour the batter into the muffin cups, filling each about 2/3 full. Bake for 18-20 minutes or until a toothpick comes out clean. Let cool before serving.

Coconut Cream Pie

Ingredients

- **For the Crust:**
    - 1 1/2 cups graham cracker crumbs
    - 1/4 cup granulated sugar
    - 1/2 cup unsalted butter, melted
- **For the Filling:**
    - 2 cups coconut milk
    - 1/2 cup granulated sugar
    - 1/4 cup cornstarch
    - 1/4 teaspoon salt
    - 3 large egg yolks, beaten
    - 1 teaspoon vanilla extract
    - 1 cup shredded coconut (sweetened or unsweetened)
- **For the Topping:**
    - 1 cup heavy whipping cream
    - 2 tablespoons powdered sugar
    - 1 teaspoon vanilla extract

Instructions

1. **Preheat Oven:** Preheat your oven to 350°F (175°C).
2. **Make the Crust:** In a bowl, combine graham cracker crumbs, sugar, and melted butter. Press mixture into the bottom and up the sides of a 9-inch pie pan. Bake for 10 minutes. Let cool.
3. **Prepare the Filling:** In a saucepan, whisk together coconut milk, sugar, cornstarch, and salt. Cook over medium heat, stirring constantly until thickened. Remove from heat, and gradually whisk in egg yolks. Stir in vanilla and shredded coconut.
4. **Assemble Pie:** Pour filling into the cooled crust. Refrigerate for at least 4 hours or until set.
5. **Make Topping:** Whip heavy cream, powdered sugar, and vanilla until soft peaks form. Spread over the pie before serving.

Bourbon Pecan Pie

Ingredients

- **For the Crust:**
    - 1 1/4 cups all-purpose flour
    - 1/4 teaspoon salt
    - 1/4 cup unsalted butter, chilled and diced
    - 1/4 cup ice water
- **For the Filling:**
    - 1 cup corn syrup
    - 1 cup brown sugar
    - 4 large eggs
    - 1/4 cup unsalted butter, melted
    - 1/4 cup bourbon
    - 1 teaspoon vanilla extract
    - 2 cups pecan halves

Instructions

1. **Preheat Oven:** Preheat your oven to 350°F (175°C).
2. **Make the Crust:** In a bowl, mix flour and salt. Cut in butter until mixture resembles coarse crumbs. Stir in ice water, a tablespoon at a time, until dough forms. Shape into a disk, wrap in plastic, and refrigerate for 30 minutes.
3. **Roll Out Dough:** Roll out dough on a floured surface to fit a 9-inch pie pan. Place in pie pan and trim edges.
4. **Prepare Filling:** In a large bowl, whisk together corn syrup, brown sugar, eggs, melted butter, bourbon, and vanilla. Stir in pecans.
5. **Assemble Pie:** Pour filling into the prepared crust.
6. **Bake:** Bake for 50-60 minutes until set. Let cool before serving.

Espresso Brownies

Ingredients

- 1/2 cup unsalted butter
- 1 cup granulated sugar
- 2 large eggs
- 1 teaspoon vanilla extract
- 1/3 cup unsweetened cocoa powder
- 1/2 cup all-purpose flour
- 1/4 teaspoon salt
- 1 teaspoon espresso powder
- 1/2 cup chocolate chips

Instructions

1. **Preheat Oven:** Preheat your oven to 350°F (175°C). Grease an 8x8-inch baking pan.
2. **Melt Butter:** In a saucepan, melt the butter. Remove from heat and stir in sugar, eggs, and vanilla.
3. **Mix Dry Ingredients:** In a separate bowl, whisk together cocoa powder, flour, salt, and espresso powder.
4. **Combine Mixtures:** Gradually add the dry mixture to the wet mixture, stirring until combined. Fold in chocolate chips.
5. **Bake:** Pour batter into the prepared baking pan and bake for 20-25 minutes. Let cool before cutting into squares.

Marble Cake

Ingredients

- 2 1/2 cups all-purpose flour
- 2 1/2 teaspoons baking powder
- 1/2 teaspoon salt
- 1 cup unsalted butter, softened
- 2 cups granulated sugar
- 4 large eggs
- 1 teaspoon vanilla extract
- 1 cup milk
- 1/2 cup unsweetened cocoa powder

Instructions

1. **Preheat Oven:** Preheat your oven to 350°F (175°C). Grease and flour a 10-inch bundt pan.
2. **Mix Dry Ingredients:** In a bowl, whisk together flour, baking powder, and salt.
3. **Cream Butter and Sugar:** In a large bowl, cream together butter and sugar until light and fluffy. Add eggs, one at a time, mixing well after each addition. Stir in vanilla.
4. **Combine Mixtures:** Gradually add dry ingredients to the butter mixture, alternating with milk.
5. **Create Marble Effect:** Divide the batter in half. Mix cocoa powder into one half. In the prepared bundt pan, alternate spoonfuls of the vanilla and chocolate batter. Use a knife to swirl the two together.
6. **Bake:** Bake for 50-60 minutes until a toothpick comes out clean. Let cool before serving.

Vanilla Pudding Cake

Ingredients

- 1/2 cup unsalted butter, melted
- 1 cup granulated sugar
- 1 cup milk
- 1 tablespoon vanilla extract
- 1 cup all-purpose flour
- 1/2 teaspoon baking powder
- 1/4 teaspoon salt
- 2 large eggs

Instructions

1. **Preheat Oven:** Preheat your oven to 350°F (175°C). Grease a 9-inch round cake pan.
2. **Mix Ingredients:** In a bowl, combine melted butter, sugar, milk, and vanilla. Whisk until smooth.
3. **Add Dry Ingredients:** Stir in flour, baking powder, and salt until combined.
4. **Add Eggs:** Beat in eggs until well combined.
5. **Bake:** Pour batter into the prepared pan and bake for 30-35 minutes until golden and set. Let cool before serving.

Chocolate Chip Pancakes

Ingredients

- 1 cup all-purpose flour
- 2 tablespoons sugar
- 1 teaspoon baking powder
- 1/2 teaspoon baking soda
- 1/4 teaspoon salt
- 1 cup buttermilk
- 1 large egg

- 2 tablespoons unsalted butter, melted
- 1/2 cup chocolate chips

Instructions

1. **Mix Dry Ingredients:** In a bowl, whisk together flour, sugar, baking powder, baking soda, and salt.
2. **Combine Wet Ingredients:** In another bowl, mix buttermilk, egg, and melted butter.
3. **Combine Mixtures:** Pour wet ingredients into dry ingredients and stir until just combined. Fold in chocolate chips.
4. **Cook Pancakes:** Heat a skillet over medium heat. Pour 1/4 cup batter onto the skillet. Cook until bubbles form on the surface, then flip and cook until golden brown. Serve warm.

Fruit and Nut Granola Bars

Ingredients

- 2 cups rolled oats
- 1/2 cup almond butter (or peanut butter)
- 1/3 cup honey (or maple syrup)
- 1/2 cup mixed nuts (chopped)
- 1/2 cup dried fruit (e.g., cranberries, apricots)
- 1/4 teaspoon salt
- 1 teaspoon vanilla extract

Instructions

1. **Preheat Oven:** Preheat your oven to 350°F (175°C). Line an 8x8-inch baking dish with parchment paper.
2. **Mix Ingredients:** In a large bowl, combine oats, almond butter, honey, chopped nuts, dried fruit, salt, and vanilla.
3. **Press Mixture:** Spread the mixture evenly into the prepared baking dish, pressing down firmly.
4. **Bake:** Bake for 20-25 minutes until golden. Let cool completely in the pan before cutting into bars.

Buttermilk Biscuits

Ingredients

- 2 cups all-purpose flour
- 1 tablespoon baking powder
- 1/2 teaspoon baking soda
- 1/2 teaspoon salt

- 1/4 cup unsalted butter, cold and diced
- 3/4 cup buttermilk

Instructions

1. **Preheat Oven:** Preheat your oven to 450°F (232°C).
2. **Mix Dry Ingredients:** In a large bowl, whisk together flour, baking powder, baking soda, and salt.
3. **Cut in Butter:** Add the cold, diced butter and cut it into the flour mixture until it resembles coarse crumbs.
4. **Add Buttermilk:** Pour in the buttermilk and stir until just combined. Do not overmix.
5. **Shape Biscuits:** Turn the dough onto a floured surface and gently knead it 3-4 times. Roll or pat the dough to about 1-inch thickness. Cut out biscuits using a biscuit cutter.
6. **Bake:** Place the biscuits on a baking sheet and bake for 12-15 minutes until golden. Serve warm.

Cherry Clafoutis

Ingredients

- 1 cup fresh or frozen cherries (pitted)
- 3 large eggs
- 1 cup milk
- 1/2 cup granulated sugar
- 1 teaspoon vanilla extract
- 1/2 teaspoon salt
- 1/2 cup all-purpose flour
- Powdered sugar for serving (optional)

Instructions

1. **Preheat Oven:** Preheat your oven to 350°F (175°C). Grease a 9-inch pie dish.
2. **Arrange Cherries:** Spread the cherries evenly in the greased dish.
3. **Mix Batter:** In a bowl, whisk together eggs, milk, sugar, vanilla, and salt. Gradually add the flour, whisking until smooth.
4. **Pour Batter:** Pour the batter over the cherries.
5. **Bake:** Bake for 35-40 minutes until puffed and golden. Let cool slightly before serving. Dust with powdered sugar if desired.

Chocolate Hazelnut Torte

Ingredients

- 1 cup hazelnuts, toasted and skinned
- 1/2 cup unsweetened cocoa powder

- 1/2 cup granulated sugar
- 1/4 teaspoon salt
- 4 large eggs
- 1/2 cup unsalted butter, melted
- 1 teaspoon vanilla extract
- Whipped cream for serving (optional)

Instructions

1. **Preheat Oven:** Preheat your oven to 350°F (175°C). Grease a 9-inch round cake pan and line the bottom with parchment paper.
2. **Process Hazelnuts:** In a food processor, blend the hazelnuts until finely ground.
3. **Mix Ingredients:** In a bowl, combine ground hazelnuts, cocoa powder, sugar, and salt. In another bowl, whisk eggs, melted butter, and vanilla. Combine the two mixtures.
4. **Bake:** Pour the batter into the prepared cake pan and bake for 25-30 minutes. Let cool before removing from the pan. Serve with whipped cream if desired.

Peanut Butter Pie

Ingredients

- **For the Crust:**
    - 1 1/2 cups graham cracker crumbs
    - 1/2 cup unsalted butter, melted
    - 1/4 cup granulated sugar
- **For the Filling:**
    - 1 cup creamy peanut butter
    - 1 cup powdered sugar
    - 1 cup heavy cream
    - 1 teaspoon vanilla extract

Instructions

1. **Preheat Oven:** Preheat your oven to 350°F (175°C).
2. **Make the Crust:** In a bowl, combine graham cracker crumbs, melted butter, and sugar. Press the mixture into the bottom of a 9-inch pie dish. Bake for 10 minutes and let cool.
3. **Prepare Filling:** In a bowl, mix peanut butter and powdered sugar until smooth. In another bowl, whip heavy cream and vanilla until soft peaks form.
4. **Combine Mixtures:** Fold the whipped cream into the peanut butter mixture until well combined.
5. **Assemble Pie:** Pour the filling into the cooled crust. Refrigerate for at least 4 hours before serving.

www.ingramcontent.com/pod-product-compliance
Lightning Source LLC
LaVergne TN
LVHW081508060526
838201LV00056BA/3008